WATER ON THE ROOF

SHANICE T ROBINSON

Water on the roof

Copyright © 2012 Shanice T Robinson

All rights reserved.

ISBN: 9798520735038

Water on the roof

To the woman
who helped me reach my level.
She knows who she is.

Water on the roof

LET'S TALK

Instagram & Twitter
@Poetshanicetr

Bliss

Q: What do you miss?

A:
I miss being a child.
I miss my innocence.
I miss my purest self.
I miss who I was before
the world got to me.

I miss when absent meant present.
I miss being imperfect & content.
I miss bird watching, before Twitter.
I miss pictures, before Instagram.
I miss ghost stories, before Snapchat.

I miss my ignorance dearly.

Water on the roof

Transparency is
the last step
toward your
strongest self.

All ice melts.

My most painful moments
are from scenarios
created in my head…

they still haven't happened.

Water on the roof

To my soulmate,

They are not me.

I want you to continue
to take a lesson from
each endeavor so that
when we fuse, it's a
fusion of our best selves.

I cannot wait to meet you
but if I have to, I will.

Love,
the one

Water on the roof

Everyone you meet is
going to chip away at you.
Some are going to decrease
you to nothing.
Some are going to create
something Michelangelo
would marvel.

The home of the brave

Oh, how sweet it is
to still find joy in a house
that is not a home for you.

Oh, how sweet it is
to still find joy in a city
that is too small for you.

Oh, how sweet it is
to still find joy a country
that has stomped on your heart
1 million times & counting.

Water on the roof

Great souls
love alike.

Q:
What makes you feel desired?
What does desire feel like?

A:
I like romantic gestures, bold ones.
I like to feel understood & calm.
I like to feel safe, I think that anyone who truly
desires you would want you to feel safe at all times.
I like to be welcomed & kept in mind.
I want to feel like a friend.
I want love, but I also want to be liked.
I like handwritten letters & just because flowers.
I like a mood setter.
I like compliments, make them random & genuine.
Hand placement is very special to me.
Touch me like you know i'm yours.
I like soft kisses & soft speaking.
I like the encouragement of my true being & quirks.
I like to feel paid attention to, every detail
from a nail color change to a beauty mark
to a facial expression—it's all noticed.
I like tight hugs where you don't want to let go.
I want our interactions to feel like examples.
I like the comfort in knowing that you will
never stop trying to woo me.

All-in-all desire is feeling seen in
addition to immense effort.

That's what desire feels like, a constant effort to
prove that you love me as much as I love myself.

Water on the roof

I want to meet
a soul so beautiful
that I have no choice
but to mirror it.

Hey you,

Forgive yourself for
authorizing treatment
less than what you
knew you deserved.
Charge it to the game,
but don't play it again.

Shanice T Robinson

I can feel every
condition of
your love.

Water on the roof

I'm not cocky
I just vibe high.

Sex appeal is
not an invitation.

Water on the roof

I can tell
if you embody light
by the way others shine
when with you.

When a woman's substance
matches what you
see on the surface
it's an entirely
different glow.

Water on the roof

I can't create a vibe
for someone else
until I master how
I vibe in solitude.

I do not & will not
accept lukewarm love,
lukewarm support.
Serve it hot
or leave me be.

Water on the roof

Anywhere
I go, I add.

I add encouragement.
I add peace.
I add happiness.
I add understanding.
I add reciprocity.
I add loyalty.
I add love.

I am a plus sign.

You're sexy.

Being intentional is sexy.
Knowing your "why" is sexy.
Having empathy is sexy.
Being grounded is sexy.

I gave you the most valuable
part of me knowing that you
weren't worthy without a gun
to my head, you took it knowing
that you weren't worthy
without a gun to yours…

Who's worse?

Water on the roof

If you ever heard
my conversations
with God about you,
you'd never doubt
yourself again.

I tasted like
blood, sweat & tears.
You consumed me anyway.
You found nourishment
in the darkest parts of me.

-Thank you

Water on the roof

Water yourself, not just to look wet-
but to saturate.

Feed yourself, not just the cravings-
but until you are full.

Water on the roof

When you water
a rose, the thorns
get wet too.

Water on the roof

Poetry isn't about the
metaphors & similes.
Poetry is the process & the
product of moving inward
feelings outward into the physical.
Shifting darkness from the
inside to sit out in the sun.
Articulating a memory to give
your mind some fresh air.
An emotion spelled out
clearly enough to read it back.
Turning a thought into
something tangible.
Something that can touch
your heart as soon as
your eyes touch it.

"Intense" people
keep your level steady.
Keep being intense.

It will weed out the
incapable & unwilling.

Water on the roof

I'm craving an
innocent love.
Love that doesn't
demand but instead
it presents itself,
waits for me to accept it-
makes sure that i'm sure
& then submerges me in it.

I'm craving an
unexpected love.
We have no idea
when it happened
but we can tell you
a million reasons
why it happened.

Water on the roof

May I fall
for you & you
cushion the blow?

You caught me
by cloud 9.
It's no surprise
that I feign
for a softer love.

Water on the roof

I'm craving a nostalgic love.
How old am I?
On the phone with
my legs crisscrossed
contemplating on what
I should say next.

"No, you hang up"

I don't ever want to hear
a dial tone on this love.

My heart is
wired beautifully.
When you meet a
heart that resembles
yours, it's a match
divinely made.

Water on the roof

The deep facade
doesn't go far with me.
I can see through the
inspirational quotes & crystals.
When your intent is dirty, those
are just accessories on a pig.

Substance & sex appeal
are a firm handshake.

Water on the roof

I knew that I was growing
when I started attracting people
that I wanted to be more like.
They weren't looking for a
savior, they were saving themselves.

I am many things
but I want to be loved as one.
I want to be loved for the equal parts
of everything included in myself.
Humor, passion & charisma all
wrapped in the softest skin with a
bow on top, presented to you in
the hopes that you'll love it.
I know that being loved like this
is possible because I would do it.

& you wouldn't have to ask twice,
if God forbid you had to ask at all.

-a hopeful romantic

Water on the roof

Since the first day you
walked into my mind,
you've been running
it ever since.

Everything around
us is a symbol.
The sun, the stars, the moon,
they're all high & bright.
If you need a reminder
of who you are, just look up.

Stand tall & shine.

Water on the roof

I can tell
who's spiritual &
who's compensating.

Beauty mark
on your face
because God
is precise.

Water on the roof

My love looks good on me.
I transform, I glow, my energy rises.

If my love looks good on me
then I know it will
makeover someone else.

Keep me in
mind at all times.
I want to be your
24/7 thought—
your prayers, your fantasies,
your daydreams & your nightmares.

Water on the roof

I know for a fact that
i'm here to inspire.
I'm here to be emulated
in the purest way.
I've had to go through what
i've been through to be the proof
& I have to elevate from that
place to still—be the proof.

Ever since I
picked myself up,
my heart doesn't drop
the same for you.

Water on the roof

The way that I would
feel getting booed off stage
is the same feeling I would
have receiving a standing ovation.

Anxiety has many faces.

My mother always told me
not to pick at a healing scab.
Sometimes closure is just
another bike to fall off of.

Do you know who you are?

You're the star
of my daydreams—
my mind revolves around you,
yet outside you
act like you're regular.
You walk around
as if you're not
a celebrity...like
you haven't been
on my mind heavy
enough to tip me.

Find someone that
turns your purpose on.
Find your personified push
& pull them closer.

I have different
relationship goals.
I'm trying to court myself,
meet me halfway.
The goal is to fall in
love with myself.

I want to love myself
as unconditionally as i've
loved those who've smeared me
with their fingerprints, lied about
all intentions, known that I was
fragile & still threw me on the
floor, watched me shatter...then
stomped on me just to be sure that
every shard was as fine as a grain of sugar.

I still saw the good in them.

Water on the roof

The goal is to see
the good in myself.
Where's the rose-colored glasses
when it comes to me?
I'm going to be empathetic towards
myself, forgiving & deliberate.

I will take myself back
after every heartbreak
until we get it right.
I'm not perfect but I try.
I'm going to give myself
the benefit of the doubt.

The goal is to give myself
chance after chance no matter
how offensive I behave.

No matter
how dark I get,
I will beam light
onto myself.

Water on the roof

I will see myself
even when I don't
feel visible.

I will
compliment myself
even when I don't
feel worthy.

Water on the roof

No matter what
my mind told me,
I will show mercy on
myself at all times.

I'm up next
on the roster for
an unlimited love.

Water on the roof

I've spent too long
envisioning love from
an outward source.

The source is me.

I'm pulling energy
from myself &
i'm plugged into
my own intensity.

Water on the roof

I want a
soul tie
with myself.

I'm going to strive for
the rest of my life to be
my own relationship goals.

Water on the roof

If I hear
"What's your favorite color?"
one more time i'm going to scream.

Instead:

What's a guilty pleasure of yours that's free & what's a guilty pleasure of yours that costs money?

If you could change 1 thing about how you were raised, what would you change?

Which birthday were you most/least excited about?

What 2 colors would you use to describe your mood towards life right now?

What's your unpopular opinion about love?

What's the most random thing you've ever done? Do you regret it?

Name a song or scent that takes you to a memory automatically.

If you got the fearlessness you had as a child back, what's the first thing you would do?

Do I match the person that you imagined?

Mindless conversation is
a luxury that I cannot afford.

If you want to
impress me,
tell me how
I boil blood
fully clothed.

Water on the roof

Tell me that you love
the way I carry myself.
Heavily crowned,
yet I walk light.

Tell me what you
like about my mind.
Tell me how bad you
want to be on it.

Water on the roof

Tell me that my class
is something that
cannot be taught.

Tell me that I remind
you of a bible verse.
Find it & read it to me.

Water on the roof

Tell me that I remind
you of a song.
Find it & sing it to me.

Tell me that
my substance
cannot be abused.

Water on the roof

Tell me what my
soul wants to hear then
watch me tell the
world about you.

She.

She surprises every day.
I love her, look at her.
Look how many rocks have been thrown at her
& now she's standing on top of them all.
I am becoming the woman of my dreams.
I am my own aesthetic.
I've daydreamed about this woman,
i've fantasized about her & she's
finally shining, thriving.
I've curated this woman & she's
surpassed what i've imagined.
I'm so proud of her.
I'm so proud of us.
She's a product of the environment I built for her.
I got my hands dirty, so she'd be clean.
She's a production of calamity & manifestation.
She's a gumbo of dedication &
her grandmother's prayers.
She's already an example of
substantial permanence.

The scariest part…
she's still not complete.

Water on the roof

The moment you act
like i'm average i'll leave
you alone to let you
feel why i'm not.

Gossip doesn't
penetrate my bubble.
My soul is too
loud to talk over.

Water on the roof

How ironic that
being set apart is the
perfect set up for success.

I know that my energy
is worth something or else
people wouldn't try to
infiltrate it so often.

Water on the roof

You are a part of
someone's self-care.

Shanice T Robinson

The best thing about purpose
is that it never goes away.
It's with you & it's forever growing.

Water on the roof

Anxious?
Pour into yourself.
Restless?
Pour into yourself.
Bored?
Pour into yourself.
Angry?
Pour into yourself.
Stressed?
Pour into yourself.

The most rewarding
project i've ever
worked on was my mind.

I don't want Popcorn.
I want Mac n Cheese.
I want comfort love.
I want what took time, measurement & effort.
I don't want prepackaged love.
I don't want love that everyone else has.
I want love that was made with love.
1 tbsp of the love of God, 1 cup
of the love of self & a sprinkle of the love of our
journey, no matter how long it takes.
I want love with no set time, just keep
checking on us until we're ready.

I want oven love, not microwaved.

Pay attention to what pours
back into you when you pour
into it, if the vibe is right it
should be automatic.

Water on the roof

Get some rest.

You are not unproductive.
You are a trying person working
tirelessly towards their future
& your body needs to catch up
with your work ethic.

BODY LANGUAGE

I almost said it,
it was on the tip of my tongue.
I thank God that you can't read my mind.
The thought of you isn't a variable, it's constant.
How many scenarios do I have to create
in my head before you get here?
I want to recreate them.
I almost said that i'm curious about
how high your voice can go.
Wondering if you could sing for me.
You're a museum, I need to look around.
I need to take it all in.
You look like you were carved,
painted & sculpted for me.
I almost said that I don't ever want to
get on your nerves, only nerve endings.
You need to let it out & I want to empty you.
You don't have to say my name, scream for God.
I am your vessel & you mirror me.
I almost said let's fill each other up with love.

Water on the roof

I almost said it.

I have a question...
What colors do you see
when your eyes roll back?
I almost said it,
it was on the tip of my tongue.
I bet your Instagram has never
seen the faces you make here.
The way you pose here is picture perfect.
I almost said that I wanted
you to put me in positions that
would make our ancestors gasp.
If I yield to you & you yield to me
nothing can stop us.
I almost said let's go.
With every stroke, you sign
one letter of your name.
Sign, sealed, delivered.
I almost said it's yours.

I almost said it.
It was right there on
the tip of my tongue.

Where you should be.

Water on the roof

Being a martyr for your
loved ones requires deep inner
communication & boundaries
or you will run dry.
It's never a negative thing to put
others first because that's the intensity
of your love, it only becomes a problem
when that intensity is never shown on yourself.

You will never forget
who gave your
love a definition.

Water on the roof

Being loved by me
is the gift that will
never stop giving.

There is a hole
in my insecurities
in the shape of you,
you make me feel beautiful.

Water on the roof

The transparent
person is who's
truly seen.

Everything
with prestige
has limitations.

Why are we scared of bugs? -

People are scared of bugs not
because of their size, but because
of their potential to hurt you, the unknown.
Yes, you're small yet you pack power & potential.
Naturally, people will be intimidated even when you
don't see why they should be.

You think you're small? think again.

I am an endorphin
releaser in all ways.
I am a healer.
I am a stress reliever.
Please do not overuse me,
I have to be spread around.

Water on the roof

No easel
could withstand
the weight of
your beauty.

I'm drawn to you
& this can't be erased.

Water on the roof

The prototype of anything
i've ever admired.
Thank you for being the
example of my greatest desire.

Not sure if I believe
in angel numbers anymore.
The amount of times
i've been let down is 444.

Water on the roof

Recycling isn't
good for the
dating environment.

What if the reason they keep
coming back is because your
orgasm is the only way they
have ever seen you truly happy?

Water on the roof

In order to get
below my neck
you need to get
in between my eyes.

No intention, no entry.

Water on the roof

Look at you,
an answered
prayer personified.

Mercury is
not in retrograde,
karma is in action.

Water on the roof

One day, I will write about love.
All of my angst turns into poetry
but one day I will write about amity.
Instead of being inspired by brokenness
I will write about how whole I feel.
Instead of dwelling on my insecurities
I will write about how thankful I am
that they have made me relatable.

Shanice T Robinson

I've cried so many times but
i've made so many people laugh.
I will write about my experience.
My creative energy is pulled from
my disappointment in other beings.
One day, I will write about the beings
that would never do that to me.

One day, I will write about you.

Water on the roof

People say that they don't like
poetry because they don't *get* it.
I write with intent.
I write for who already understands.
This is for people of substance.

Therefore, if you don't get it,
you probably don't have it.

Dress like Whitley.
Study like Kim.
Hustle like Lena.
Love like Freddie.

- *a different world*

Water on the roof

I want you badly because
I want what's best for me.

I know the difference between
checking in & checking
the temperature.

It's still hot.

Let's recreate Loves Jones
minus the mixed signals.
Our version will be clear,
just passion & poetry.

- *One wish*

Stopping to give yourself
flowers doesn't stop progression.
Every journey has pit stops, take
them unapologetically.

Water on the roof

God believes in you.
I believe in you.
I hope that makes 3 of us.

The love has
to feel like a neo-soul
song on repeat.

Water on the roof

I will not water myself down
so that you can feel me.
Your insecurity around a force
is none of the force's business.
I do not dilute.
Take it all at its intensity
or get nothing.

I thank God for denying
me the things that I prayed for.
I wanted things that
were unfulfilling, unaligned
& held no reciprocity.

Water on the roof

I've dodged so many
bullets meanwhile,
I prayed for the gun.

Google the meaning of Invictus.
Now, go look in the mirror.

Water on the roof

If it has no intent or sense
of direction for the betterment
of myself & itself, I pray that
God steers me clear.

I want your
horror &
your romcom.

Water on the roof

I don't own anyone
or their time.
I'm forever thankful
for anything given to me.

THE CONVERSATION

Anxiety likes conversation & long walks on the mind.

Anxiety sneaks up on you & asks you a few questions:

"*wyd*?" but not in the fuckboy kind of way.
What are you doing with your life?

It goes away & then it comes back with some more questions:

"*Who are you*?" but not in the amnesia kind of way.
Who are you without the makeup, the clothes or the job?

"*Where are you*?" but not in the mom kind of way.
Where are you? I mean, look around at all of this failure.

"*How are you*?" but not in the friend kind of way.
How are you even happy right now?

Are you happy?

If your answer was yes, anxiety will change that for you.

If you wrote down what you were thankful for i'm sure you'd put:

1. Food
2. Shelter
3. Family & friends
4. Life

Anxiety & gratitude
do not mix well.

Anxiety wants to talk about what people think about you. Anxiety wants every detail & every encounter dissected. Playing scenarios back in your head over & over, think about what you could've done better.

Anxiety wants to talk about everything that you want to do, that you haven't done yet. It will whisper in your ear *"You can't do it. It's not time yet. It's not perfect, therefore it will fail. Stop thinking about that."*

Anxiety is a subject changer.

Anxiety will ask
you if you can swim
while it's holding
your head down.

Anxiety is a prankster.

Water on the roof

I overthink until I sink so
if you're drowning i've been there.

Under water, i've learned to take
what my anxiety says with nothing at all.
You take what people say with
a grain of salt until 1 grain is 1,000.
Those grains you took will be heavy
enough to shatter you one grain at a time.
You'd be surprised how heavy it can get.
Bones start cracking & skin starts ripping.

Anxiety is body compactor.

My mind went back & forth
with itself under the weight of
it all & nobody reached for my hand.
Nobody pulled me up because nobody
noticed I was down there.

I had to climb.

The reason why I am
so strong is because
I lifted this weight
on my own.
Believe it or not
i've breathed under
water & I just kept swimming.

There isn't an
Instagram filter
for ugly intentions.

Water on the roof

The trick up
my sleeve
is God.

I am the creator of
what i've never seen.

Water on the roof

I want
multiple
streams
of love.

Your healing
is a flower
& it is worth pruning.

Water on the roof

A closed vessel
is the saddest story.

Live & date
out of respect
for your higher self.

Water on the roof

The love inside of me
was built from the ground up.
I move with love because
moving without it would
be rock bottom.

I will not go back.

Anyone in
the comfort
zone gets towed.

Water on the roof

I love my silence.
It's louder than anyone
could scream & a storm
always follows.

Shanice T Robinson

There's more to life than
what we do to escape it.
Spend time with your family,
love on your friends, ask those
deep questions, be passionate
& intentional about
everything that you do.

Be remembered for compassion,
authenticity, generosity & loyalty.

Be bigger.

Made in the USA
Columbia, SC
08 August 2021